FISH

by Sophie Geister-Jones

Cody Koala

An Imprint of Pop!
popbooksonline.com

abdobooks.com

Published by Pop!, a division of ABDO, PO Box 398166, Minneapolis, Minnesota 55439. Copyright © 2020 by POP, LLC. International copyrights reserved in all countries. No part of this book may be reproduced in any form without written permission from the publisher. Pop!™ is a trademark and logo of POP, LLC.

Printed in the United States of America, North Mankato, Minnesota

102019
012020

THIS BOOK CONTAINS RECYCLED MATERIALS

Cover Photo: OJO Images Ltd/Alamy
Interior Photos: OJO Images Ltd/Alamy, 1; iStockphoto, 5, 7 (top), 7 (bottom left), 7 (bottom right), 8, 9, 11, 13, 14, 15, 17 (top), 17 (bottom left), 17 (bottom right), 18–19, 20, 21

Editor: Meg Gaertner
Series Designer: Sophie Geister-Jones

Library of Congress Control Number: 2019942760

Publisher's Cataloging-in-Publication Data

Names: Geister-Jones, Sophie, author
Title: Fish / by Sophie Geister-Jones
Description: Minneapolis, Minnesota : Pop!, 2020 | Series: Pets | Includes online resources and index.
Identifiers: ISBN 9781532165702 (lib. bdg.) | ISBN 9781532167027 (ebook)
Subjects: LCSH: Aquarium fishes--Juvenile literature. | Fishes as pets--Juvenile literature. | Pets--Juvenile literature. | Fishes--Behavior--Juvenile literature.
Classification: DDC 639.34--dc23

Hello! My name is

Cody Koala

Pop open this book and you'll find QR codes like this one, loaded with information, so you can learn even more!

Scan this code* and others like it while you read, or visit the website below to make this book pop.

popbooksonline.com/fish

*Scanning QR codes requires a web-enabled smart device with a QR code reader app and a camera.

Table of Contents

Behavior

Fish live in the water. They are almost always moving. In the wild, many fish live in **schools**. Schools of fish swim together.

Watch a video here!

History

People in China kept wild fish in ponds in the 800s. Over time, these fish became **domesticated**. By the 1500s, many people in China kept pet goldfish in bowls.

Learn more here!

Goldfish are one of the most common types of pet fish today. Pet goldfish are often yellow, gold, or orange.

betta fish

People also keep guppies, betta fish, and other kinds.

Fish have been around for more than 500 million years.

Chapter 3

Many Types of Fish

There are more than 25,000 **species** of fish. Some fish live in salt water. Others live in fresh water. Not all fish make good pets.

Learn more here!

People have many good options for pet fish. Pet fish come in different sizes. Some are very small. Others are big. But all pet fish have similar body parts.

Some fish sleep by floating in place.

mouth

eye

dorsal fin

gills

tail fin

Pet fish come in many
different colors. Some
have brown or gray **scales**.

Others are bright yellow or blue. **Male** and **female** fish might be different colors.

Chapter 4

Fish Care

Pet fish live in tanks. Owners must fill the tank with the right kind of water. Different fish may need cold or warm water. They may need salty or fresh water.

Complete an activity here!

Some fish eat meat. Some eat plants. Others eat both. Owners can find the right food for their pet fish at a pet store.

Some fish can be trained to swim toward a sound or eat from a person's hand.

Fish need space to swim
and explore. A tank should
have plants and rocks.

Fish can hide behind them.
Owners should also clean
the tank regularly.

Making Connections

Text-to-Self

Do you know someone who has a pet fish? What color is it? What does it eat?

Text-to-Text

Have you read other books about fish? What did you learn?

Text-to-World

Why do you think people like having fish as pets?

Glossary

domesticated – tame or kept as a pet.

female – a person or animal of the sex that can have babies or lay eggs.

male – a person or animal of the sex that cannot have babies or lay eggs.

scale – one of many thin, flat, overlapping plates that cover the bodies of fish.

school – a group of fish that swim together.

species – a group of animals of the same kind that can have babies together.

Index

Online Resources

popbooksonline.com

Thanks for reading this Cody Koala book!

Scan this code* and others like it in this book, or visit the website below to make this book pop!

popbooksonline.com/fish

*Scanning QR codes requires a web-enabled smart device with a QR code reader app and a camera.